SAINT FRANCIS

BRIAN WILDSMITH

I was born, thank you, God, over eight hundred years ago.
And still I live in people's hearts.
I loved my name — Francis. I loved my city — Assisi.
And I loved my life.

My delight was to sing and play the lute,
to wear fine clothes, to joke with my friends,
and to dance with them all through the countryside.

One day the bells of Assisi pealed out in anger:
'The city of Perugia is about to attack.
Take up arms and fight!'

I longed for fame and glory.
I put on my shining armour and rode into battle.
We were defeated, and I was captured.
Laden down with chains, I was dragged to Perugia.

The prison was cold and damp. My fellow prisoners were sad.
They never laughed, they never sang.
And so I sang to them. I joked with them and made them laugh.
But I became ill, and I too became sad.
My father paid a ransom for me, and I went home to Assisi.

My mother nursed me back to health, but still I was sad.
Spring arrived and I went out walking.
The sun shone, but I did not see it.
The birds sang, but I did not hear.
Flowers filled the air with scent, but I was unaware.

I came to the ruined church of San Damiano and knelt to pray. I heard a voice:
'Francis, my church is falling into ruin. Go and repair it for me.'
I saw the sun, I heard the birds, I smelt the flowers, I danced.
God had spoken to me.

To repair the church, I stole money from my father.
He was angry and dragged me before the Bishop.
'Give your father back the money you stole,' said the Bishop.
'Yes, my Lord,' I said. 'And that's not all I will do.
Look, I'm giving him back not just his money,
but all the clothes that he gave me.'

I threw off all my clothes and laid them at my father's feet.
And then I turned my back on them all and walked
out of the city gates, singing for joy.

From then on, I sought out the poor.
I sought out the sick.
I repaired God's ruined churches.
I loved all God's creatures and
called them my brothers and sisters.

One day I heard a priest read these words from the Bible:
'Go out and tell the people the Good News about God.
Don't take any money. Don't wear any shoes.
Don't carry a staff. Just go.'
I knew then what I had to do. I walked from city to town.
I told everybody about the beauty of the world.
I told the people that God loved them.
A rich man called Bernard gave away everything he owned to
the poor. He came to join me, and many others followed him.

We talked to everyone and everything that would listen to us.
One day I saw a great flock of birds in a meadow.
'My little brothers and sisters,' I said, 'God loves you.
He has given you wings and beautiful feathers.
He has made you free to fly
wherever you want. It is your duty
to sing to God all day long.'
The birds all opened their beaks
and beat their wings together.
I blessed them and they flew
up into the sky, all singing.

I walked to Rome and saw the Pope.
There he was in his fine church with all the priests dressed up
in their fine robes.

I told him stories, I sang him songs, I told him how good it was
to be poor. I asked him to bless all that I was doing.
The Pope smiled and gave me his blessing, and I danced for joy.

I had a friend, a childhood friend.
Her name was Clare.
Her heart was as pure as gold.
She came by moonlight
with her maid to see me.

She said:
'My love will shine like a beacon
Across land and sea
To show people the way to you and to God.
Wherever you go, my love will follow you.
Wherever you are, you will not be alone.
I will stay with you for ever.'

There was fighting in the Holy Land.
I had to go there to try and stop people killing each other.
All my followers wanted to come. I did not know which to choose.
So I asked a little child to choose twelve for me,
and we sailed to the Holy Land.

A great battle was about to start. I begged them not to fight.
But they took no notice. Thousands of men were killed.
I felt as though my heart was frozen.
I felt as though I was weeping tears of ice,
and I returned to Assisi.

One Christmas Eve at Greccio I made
a Christmas scene so that ordinary people
could understand the mystery of Christ's birth.
I brought in a real ox and an ass. I had real people
to play the parts of Mary and Joseph and the shepherds.
And there was a real manger with a real baby in it.
Crowds of people came from all the villages
to see the wonderful Nativity.

I went to a mountain to pray,
close by where Brother Eagle had built his nest.
Early one morning the beating of his wings woke me from sleep.

The sky was ablaze and a vision of wonder appeared.
My hands, my feet — they felt as though they were pierced
with nails, and a wound appeared in my side.
I felt that the Gates of Paradise were opening for me.

I came to Gubbio where there was a savage wolf.
I went out to meet him and he rushed at me, snarling.
'Brother Wolf,' I said, 'you have done great harm.
But it was only because you were hungry. If now you
agree to live in peace with the people, I will ask them
always to give you food.'
The wolf wagged his tail and gave me his paw.
And all the people cheered and promised to feed
Brother Wolf for ever.

When the sun touched my eyes, it spoke to me
no more, for I had become blind and ill.
I was taken to the Bishop's Palace in Assisi
and Clare came to take care of me.

But everyone was so sad. I sang them the
Song of Brother Sun to cheer them up.
But I wanted to leave this grand palace.
'Take me back to my little church
outside Assisi,' I asked.

Very gently I was carried to my little church.
'Stop,' I said as we left the city gates. 'Turn me towards Assisi.'
I could not see my beloved Assisi but I could feel it. I blessed
it and all the people who would come to it in the future.
We arrived at the little church. I knew the sun was about to set.
An exultation of larks flew over, singing in glory as I walked
through the Gates of Paradise.

Saint Francis

Francis was born in the Italian town of Assisi in 1181. His father was a wealthy cloth-merchant. Francis helped him run the business and passed his leisure time singing and dancing with his friends.

In a war between Assisi and Perugia, Francis was captured and held in prison for a year. He became ill, and was ransomed by his father. When he came home he heard a voice which seemed to come from the crucifix in the ruined church of San Damiano: 'Go and repair my house, which is falling down.'

To get money for the repairs, Francis stole some scarlet cloth from his father and sold it. His father was furious and dragged him before the Bishop. Francis renounced his father by stripping off all his clothes in public and began a new life.

He rebuilt San Damiano and started to repair other churches. One day he heard a priest read from the Bible the instructions given by Jesus to his disciples. Francis then became a travelling preacher, owning nothing but his coat and begging for food. He always referred to himself as *il poverello* — the little poor man. He loved the whole of creation and preached in simple language to people, animals, and birds.

In 1210 with the permission of the Pope he set up a new order of 'friars' (brothers). There were just twelve at first, committed to a life of poverty, obedience, and prayer. An order for women was set up by his friend Clare in 1212.

Francis went to the Holy Land in 1219 but was unable to stop the fighting. He met the Sultan, who was impressed by Francis' sincerity.

Francis was a very devout man and while praying on Mount La Verna he had a vision and found on his body the stigmata — the scars of the wounds of Christ. Soon after this, Francis fell seriously ill and became blind. In the midst of his sufferings he wrote 'The Canticle of Brother Sun', praising all God's creatures. He died in 1226, aged only forty-five. The Franciscan Order has taken his message of love, joy, and peace to the four corners of the world.